YOU DON'T KNOW SPIT

DR. SCOTT MENAKER

Copyright © 2018 by Dr. Scott Menaker

All rights reserved. This book may not be reproduced or stored in whole or in part by any means without the written permission of the author except for brief quotations for the purpose of review.

ISBN: 978-1-943258-80-2

Edited by: Elizabeth Russell

Published by WARREN Publishing
Charlotte, NC
www.warrenpublishing.net
Printed in the United States

To my father, who instilled in me an insurmountable drive for success, my brother Steve, who has challenged me my whole life, and to the best wingman in the world, my wife Pam, who knows how to push the right buttons to get the best out of me. And last but not least, to my mom and my three sons, who bring me joy each and every day.

OPEN WIDE

We, as a people and as a society, have a tendency to over-think and over-complicate things. We mull things over, do research, talk to friends, talk to consultants, go online, visit review sites, and ruminate on things until we are totally confused. Then we search the internet and get even more great information, and just when we're ready to make a decision, we search again. We ask others to help us make decisions, and even go as far as to let them decide for us. And then we either can't act or make decisions for the wrong reasons.

The purpose of this book is simple—to help you cut through the unimportant stuff, stop wasting time, and get to the point. So, here goes.

Life is just not that complicated. Be nice, be truthful, be honest, help others, and be considerate. Be smart and knowledgeable, and spend time reading and learning your entire life. Love your family, your children, and your friends; treat your patients and employees like family (they earn it); and help make the world a better place. And most importantly, slow down. We are always in a hurry, with technology making everything happen in an instant. Being in a rush is sometimes necessary, but many times we speak too quickly, act and react without all the facts, and don't take time to appreciate the moment. Slowing down isn't too complicated, is it? Yet somehow, we manage to make everything a lot harder than it has to be.

I initially thought about writing this book just for the dental industry, but the more I wrote down my thoughts and ideas, the more I realized that they apply to all people, no matter what they do. After all, business is business and sound principles apply no matter what your job is. So, while the book may have stories or ideas drawn from the dental world in which I work, the principles apply to any job or profession. Follow these principles, and your work *and* play lives will be much smoother, more successful, and less complicated. And a heck of a lot more fun!

And then there is the question of whether my advice applies to a certain age group or not. I would offer that it is best and easier if begun early in our adult lives. Building good habits and maintaining them is much simpler than trying to take ideas that we have accepted as gospel for decades and change them.

I have three sons, Nate, Max, and Ari, all of whom I have tried to guide and influence to my way of thinking. Brainwashing might have been easier, but I never gave up. My sons might call it torture, but as a parent, there is nothing like putting up the good fight even when we sometimes lose. What I have found with my sons is that time was the real key to understanding and accepting some of the good, sound ideas that seemed irrational to them just a few years before. This is exactly what I did with my father's advice, much of which I only appreciated later in my life. Their brains just needed some time to process; they needed to have experiences before they could move to the next level of control in their lives. I was no different from them and neither are you. Don't worry, that's just how life is. We do get older and wiser.

Let me tell you about the day the lightbulb went off for my oldest son, Nate. I received an email from Nate one day with a link to a YouTube video and the message, "Hey Dad, check out this video. It is about all the stuff you are always talking about." Off I go to YouTube to find a TED talk video. TED talks are concise and stimulating twenty-minute presentations about anything and everything. (I could give you much more detail on these talks, but I encourage you to check them out for yourself). So, I go to the TED talk given by Simon Sinek titled *Start with*

Why. Well, Nate was right on target. It is a great video, right up my alley, and I still recommend that people watch it. I have used this video with my staff and it is a critical part of my business thought process. The best part is I never would have found it without Nate. At some point, our many discussions about life, decision making, etc., had registered and hit home with him. We even attended a TED talk event in Charlotte together. As a twenty-year-old, Nate understood that what I was saying would help him to thrive a little faster and more easily. That is my hope for you too, as you read this book.

Let me clarify one thing before I go on. There are times life does get complicated. Usually we cause it to be that way, and then we need to deal with it. I have been in those situations and it was my own doing, so I understand completely how things can get away from you. How we deal with problems is the key. This book will go a long way toward helping you keep things fairly straightforward in your life, and may also help you deal with any complications you face. I want you to enjoy life and enjoy what you do every day.

A dentist will always tell you to "open wide," and that's what I want you to do now. I want you to open everything as wide as you can to take everything in, process it, and then make good decisions. Open your ears and hear everything around you. Actually pause and listen instead of having preconceived ideas about what others are saying or going to say. Open your eyes and see what is going on. Open your mind and don't let the world hold you back. And lastly, only open your mouth after you have taken it all in, so your words are well-chosen and effective. These are my keys to keeping your professional life and your personal life as uncomplicated as you can make them.

Putting the book to work for YOU

Not everything can happen all at the same time. There are just not enough hours in the day. But taking positive steps each and every day will help you move in the right direction.

> *"Lay one perfect brick every day."*
> –WILL SMITH

I have tried to keep the book's format simple and easy to follow. I will detail key topics, discuss them and clarify my thinking, give you key takeaways to focus on, and give you some action steps you can take to help uncomplicate your world. I'll pose questions that will hopefully help you slow down and consider things a little more clearly and thoughtfully. This will lead to one thing: a better you, no matter where the world takes you!

CONTENTS

1	Slow Down (Just a Little)	1
2	Two Questions to Ask Yourself	8
3	WHY?	16
4	Life's Two Big Problems, And Yours Too, If You Let Them…	20
5	Vision	29
6	Goals	37
7	Who are You Running With?	45
8	Loyalty: Your Own Multi-Level Marketing Organization	51
9	"How" Will Define Your Business	58
10	Numbers Don't Lie	62
11	Who's Driving Your Train?	66
12	Knowledge and Innovation	71
13	Looking Forward	77
14	It's All About the Relationships	81
15	Consultants	86
16	Have Fun	90
17	So, Now What?	95

SLOW DOWN
(JUST A LITTLE)

In today's hectic and fast-paced world, we are always told to speed up or get left behind. If you don't keep up with the latest in technology, you'll miss out. Go, go, go, go, go. People honk the horn to make sure you keep pace with the car in front, even if you are in bumper-to-bumper traffic. The list is endless. And I haven't even mentioned the smartphone, which has given us the world at our fingertips.

In my very busy dental practice, time is crucial. My work day is about being and staying on time. Many days, I have my staff waiting on me, some procedures are not going according to plan, and now I am running behind and ... the clock is ticking. The tendency is to speed up in situations such as these. Your blood pressure rises and the urge to hurry and get things done increases. You start to feel the beads of sweat on your brow as your fight-or-flight mechanism takes control. We have all been there and the best thing you can do is ... slow down. Take a deep breath and plan your next steps instead of allowing the pressure to force you to do things you normally would not do.

I am a stickler for running on time. Time is crucial to me in every part of my life. I wear a watch and always have. My sons don't wear watches even though they all have nice ones. They just pull their phones out (I guess I should say their mobile command centers) and show me the huge display when I ask them about the time. But I think there's something more to it. A watch reminds me of the importance of time. Time is valuable.

I have attended numerous continuing education courses over the years that focus on time. We are told not to waste precious seconds in order to maximize time and profits. If you cut fifteen seconds on *this* procedure and you do it 300 times a year, you can have another seventy-five minutes to do more dentistry. For some people, cutting time is the ultimate way to practice, but I disagree. I work quickly and efficiently, but I don't fret over a minute here and a couple more minutes there. I would much rather spend five minutes talking with a patient and working on building and maintaining a good relationship. And I want my staff to do the same thing. As you will see later in the book, fostering relationships is one of the keys to long-term success, no matter what you do.

I hate cancellations and open time, but I find productive things to do during unexpected down time. I might pay bills, review statistics and trends on how things are going in the practice, catch up on lab work, or I might even just throw my feet on the desk and read a journal or search the internet for new things happening in dentistry or around the world.

But driving yourself and your staff crazy over lost seconds is clearly one way to *not* have fun. Slow down a little and enjoy your patients (or friends, family, co-workers—whoever) and your interactions with them. It is amazing how much you will learn about people and life by just engaging with all the wonderful people who come through your door.

People notice when you are rushed, even though you may do everything in your power to look cool, calm, and collected. My heart skips a beat when patients say things like, "You must be really busy today" or "They've got you running around today, don't they?" I want people to think I am concentrating my efforts on them and creating value for the money they're paying me, and I feel like I lose that when I'm rushed, or it's perceived that way.

I'm a big fan of telling people to slow down and let the world catch up. I spent my high school and college summers working at Carowinds, a large amusement park in Charlotte, NC, where I grew up and still live. One of the perks of working there (it was not the less than minimum wage they were allowed to pay us) was free attendance at the concerts. There was a concert every weekend, and many national artists came through Carowinds. Jimmy Buffett and his Coral Reefer Band were regulars every year and always set the record for most beer sold per show. One night, the crowd was excited and kept chanting for Jimmy Buffett to play his famous hit, *Margaritaville*. Jimmy just smiled and laughed and replied, "All in the goodness of time." He would then play a different song and the crowd would repeat its chants and he would again repeat, "All in the goodness of time." He built the crowd into a frenzy, which served his purpose but also gave the crowd something to wait for. I repeat this story often because it really relates to our everyday lives. We are usually in such a hurry and want immediate satisfaction. I think we miss out on a lot of things in our rush for instant gratification, and the key thing we omit is *fun*. Slow down and enjoy where you are, who you are with, and the time at hand.

Today's business world is all about seizing the moment and maximizing efforts and pace. I could not agree more. But it is imperative not to lose the focus on your ultimate goals: to provide a great service with attention to detail—and to keep people coming back for more. For that to happen, patients need to feel like they are important to us and that our time and focus is on them. One of the biggest changes in dentistry in my over thirty-year career has been the changes in dental insurance to a PPO model, where dentists agree to take decreased compensation for being on the insurance "provider list." This has created a difficult dynamic because it requires dentists to see more patients in the same period of time in order to stay even financially.

A young dentist friend of mine started a practice and came out of the gates at a full sprint. So far, so good. His focus was to get everyone in the door. An orderly schedule was not a priority. He was busy and successful. Well, kind of. He had lots of people coming in the door, with little time to even breathe. His staff was stressed and burnt out after a short period of time, his patients were not coming back for follow-up visits, and new patients would come in the door and leave before being seen because of long wait times and his chaotic schedule. My recommendation to him was "slow down." I told him, "Your right arm can only be in one room at a time." It can be hard to do, but being smart about how you manage your time is crucial to your long-term success.

I have not always been so good with my personal time, and my wife, Pam, has helped me recognize this. I am all about giving my time to my practice, to my community, to my family, to my consulting business, etc. And on top of that, I am a lousy sleeper and, unfortunately, have too many great creative moments in the middle of the night. I take very little time for myself. I have met very few causes I feel are not worthy of my time. I spent over twenty-five years on the board of the Jewish Community Center of Charlotte, and have also served on the national JCC Association board. I served on many other committees in our community, including a non-profit community board that helps find access to health care for people who have nowhere else to turn. The list goes on and I realize I am not alone—many of us commit ourselves to things we feel are important. That is really a great thing, both personally and for the communities in which we live. But there has to be a limit. I finally stepped away from the local JCC board, allowed other board commitments to lapse, and have said "not at this time" to other requests. I'm slowing down just a little, but I think it will improve my efforts, concentration, and results in the things I do take on.

The best advice I've ever received regarding slowing down came from Nick, my caddie during a 2015 golf trip in Scotland with my buddies. The first nine holes were great, with the wind at my back and the ball going where I wanted it to, but I was only halfway done with my round. My hope for a great back nine soon faded as we turned for home and faced twenty-mile-per-hour winds. Everything was disrupted. My tempo was off, it was hard to concentrate as the wind became a huge distraction, and my great round was disintegrating in front of me.

> *"In Scotland, we have a saying,*
> *'When it's breezy, swing easy.'"*
> –Nick the Caddie

After a few holes of watching me make bad shots and hunt for my wayward golf balls, Nick offered me some sage advice. He told me the wind had changed my game and I was trying too hard and swinging too fast as I tried to compensate. Nick's advice hit home, and my game improved as I slowed down, took my time, and let my natural swing take over. This is the same thing that happens in the business world, like links golf in Scotland, our lives are no different in that slowing down can be the best medicine to cure our stress and our problems. When facing difficulties, no matter where you are and what you are doing, take a moment to slow yourself down. The solutions and answers will be clearer and the obstacles easier to overcome.

KEY TAKEAWAY: Life can get breezy. Take time to slow down and you will find more enjoyment and fewer headaches.

One of the most common things I say in my office and elsewhere is "slow down." I talk more slowly, lower the volume of my voice, and say less. It is amazing to watch the faces of my team members change as I talk with them, and, more importantly, it is amazing to see how much it improves their responses and ability to handle the situation. The same works with patients as I try to settle them down, calm their nerves, and help them handle difficult situations.

ACTION STEP: Spend some quiet time when you are not in the office thinking about what goes on in your business and/or personal life on a daily basis. Think about five things you can "slow down" that will have a positive effect on you and the job you do. Then, gradually implement these changes into your routine. I predict you will see a more productive and energetic you as a result of this one small change.

TWO QUESTIONS TO ASK YOURSELF

Your success in almost anything you do comes down to two questions. Answer these with conviction, thought, and clarity, and you will be well on your way to achieving your goals and creating success in almost everything you do.

1. What are you selling?
2. Why you?

It gets no simpler than that.

The word "sell" gets such a bad rap. The usual suspects that have contributed to this are car salesmen, telemarketers, or anyone paid on commission. These folks have one vision and goal: to get paid. The only way to do that is to make a sale. I certainly have had a not-so-good experience or two buying a car, but not all salesmen are created equal. There are plenty of great ones out there. We think of selling as some pushy salesperson who will not take "no" for an answer. Or our minds go to direct marketing salespeople who get you on the phone and do not let go no matter what you say. The key in selling is your approach and how you deliver your message.

What are you selling?

Everyone sells something. It doesn't matter what field you work in; we all sell something. I sell dentistry. I sell cleanings, crowns, dentures, etc. Every other dentist in town sells the same things, more or less.

Or do they?

And are cleanings, etc. *all* I sell? No, because I sell a lot more than just dental services. I sell health and wellness, products and service, and, most importantly, the great care of my entire team built on trust and relationships. I sell comfort. I sell it in a special way that builds friendships, loyal patients, and value. If you think about your business as a commodity, you are no different from anyone else. You can be the PPO practice, the discount denture clinic, or a Medicaid office, attracting patients based on fees alone. You may think the only thing that separates you from another dentist is price. Let's leave that mindset to the value stores of the world. It is a terrible idea to base your success on fees alone, because there is no long-term foundation to ensure this continues. Thinking you will only survive if your price is right won't get you very far. What you offer must be more than that. Your business is much more likely to thrive based on the service, care, and technical skills you offer, and not solely on low fees.

Recently, there was word from a fellow dentist in my community who closed his doors due to bankruptcy. While I don't know all the details, he described the main causes as a downturn in the economy and a competitive market. In reality, he did not position his practice for success and probably lost track of what he was selling and how to do it to generate a profit.

There are many low-cost clinics that accept all reduced-fee insurance plans and Medicaid. They serve a purpose in our communities. Most dental offices will see pro bono patients in their practices because it is a part of what we do and who we are. It is something we should and must do to help those in need who have nowhere else to turn. But I have invested a tremendous amount of time, effort, and money to create a practice that goes above and beyond the baseline of standard care. I want people to talk about how great things are in my practice and how well we treat them. I don't want to be known as the cheapest in town because that's not the type of practice I've built. I have invested a lot of money and profits back into our practice in technology and in the types of dental services that we provide to our patients. I want to be known for the terrific services we provide *and* for doing it at a fair price. So, understand what you're selling, and then do a great job selling it.

Every business has clients and patients who come in for a second opinion or to compare what they've heard from another business. Stop and ask yourself, "Why are they here?" Simply, it is a lack of trust and a failure to understand what they are buying and from whom they are buying it. I see people all the time for second opinions. I am disappointed in the amount of treatment that is proposed or "being sold" to patients that is unnecessary. Don't underestimate the patient's perception of what is going on. They recognize when they are being "sold" something.

> *"People do not want to be sold;*
> *they want to buy."*
> –JEFFREY GITOMER, INTERNATIONAL SALES TRAINER

Give your patients (or clients, or customers) a reason to buy from you and stop trying to sell them something they either don't want or don't need. I know there is more than one way to treat a patient's perceived needs, but some of this goes beyond up-selling and it is plainly wrong.

The word "selling" is given a bad rap because it's misunderstood. Selling should not involve high-pressure pitches and scare tactics. Selling is about education and understanding a client's wants and needs; it's about giving people a reason to buy from you. It is an honest discussion built on trust. When talking with patients, they will listen, but they are tuned to only one station, WIFM—What's in It For Me? Answer this question for your patient in a truthful and compassionate way and then stop talking and let them say yes. My favorite statement when presenting treatment plans or making recommendations is to tell patients, "This is what I would do for my mother, wife, or children, and I love them."

> **KEY TAKEAWAY:** Ask better questions. There is only one way to truly find out what customers want, and it is probably different for each person. So, it's necessary to ask better questions. Asking questions instead of telling people what you think they want will create a great dynamic, giving people a reason to buy.

Why You?

The second question you must ask in order to achieve your goals is, why you? That's because it's all about the relationship. I think our success in dentistry is ninety-eight percent relationship and two percent service-related. It is for me. It is imperative for long-term success to establish an honest relationship with each patient. This is why they come to see you. It's not the technical quality of the dentistry I provide, because they have no way to judge that. Rather, it's because they like me and my team and the way they are treated.

I attended a continuing education course almost twenty-five years ago, and one thing I learned has stuck with me all these years. It was stated that ninety percent of what we do in dentistry is elective. Patients only need me when they break a front tooth or are in pain. How true. No matter how hard I try to prevent it, I still see patients with untreated decay, missing and broken teeth, and even no teeth. And some of them do not come to have this treated.

My first denture patient when I was a student spent three months waiting for me to make his perfect set of teeth, and he was thrilled with the results. I went through the standard instructions and told him he would hopefully soon eat a steak. He gave me a serious look and said he had eaten a steak the night before. He didn't *need* the dentures. I think he got the dentures to make his wife happy.

The longer I practice dentistry, the more I realize the importance of building strong relationships with my patients and clients. It is something that I work very hard at and I believe it's the biggest reason I have been successful. There are lots of technically great dentists who fail to be successful, and it has everything to do with their lack of people skills. Do not ignore this very important and fun part of your practice.

So remember, no matter how wonderful the services and the results turn out, dentistry is an elective, discretionary expense based on our patient's wants and needs, as are most businesses. It doesn't really matter what we think. Some patients would rather have a great car or take expensive vacations while they let other things lapse. Some patients would rather just not do the treatment they know they need. That is clearly their option. Find out what they want, help them understand the benefits and value of your services, and then let them decide how they want to proceed.

Let me tell you about my patient, John. John came in as a new patient with a deep periodontal pocket about nine millimeters deep around tooth #19, with extensive bone loss on the back side of the tooth. Figuring that John was going to need a bone graft and some extensive periodontal treatment to save the tooth, I referred him to my favorite periodontist. John's reaction was, "If it ain't broke, don't fix it." Well, I told John it was broken pretty badly and that he really needed to take care of this problem. John eventually took care of it—when he finally allowed me to remove the tooth about eight months later. Initially, John wasn't buying anything I was selling, and it was probably due to the fact he just didn't know me well enough to trust me or didn't want to trust me, or maybe I didn't help him understand the importance of what I was recommending.

Now, after twenty years of good care, John follows my advice, but he learned a hard lesson. If you help your patients understand what you're "selling," the true benefits to their health, and also establish an honest relationship, you create a loyal patient who will almost always follow your advice, *and* come back year after year.

Why should someone do business with you? What sets you apart from anyone else? Why should someone hire you? What attributes do you bring to the table that make you stand out? These are crucial questions, with even more important answers, that will define your success.

ACTION STEP: Take some quiet time and really answer the two simple questions that I posed at the beginning of this chapter: 1) What are you selling, and 2) Why You? Spend some time reviewing your answers and put them into a form you can express to someone else. When you can answer them clearly, articulate those responses to your staff, and express them to your patients in conversation and in action, you will have started down the path to success.

In almost all my interactions as a consumer, I look at these two questions. What are they selling and why them? We have so many choices in life that we can become overwhelmed by the options. Make it simple for yourself and for your patients. You will "sell" them what they need and they will "buy" from you with very little effort.

Also, spend some time reviewing and reading books and articles on the right way to sell. And check out Jeffrey Gitomer's website, Gitomer.com. Jeffrey provides some great info on how to successfully help your patients want to buy from you.

WHY?

One of the most impactful books or videos that I have read or viewed is called *Start with Why* by Simon Sinek. As I recommended to you in my introduction, I urge you to go to YouTube and search for this Simon Sinek TED talk. It will be the most eye-opening eighteen minutes of your business life. And if you want more, read the book. Let me tell you *why!*

As we make plans, set goals and embark on a working career, we are concerned with what, how, and then when. *Why* seems to be the last on the list because it is more intuitive, not one of the measurable, concrete steps or actions we are used to taking. We all learn in different ways, and I am a "why" learner. I fail when I do not understand why I am doing things.

"Why?" can be the most frustrating question you hear as a young parent from your toddler. We tell them to stop, to not do certain things, to eat their food, etc., and the first word out of their mouths is, "Why?" Even when you explain things, they still ask "Why?" As parents, we recognize their brains are not developed enough to fully understand. But I find it interesting that soon enough, they stop asking why, and I am not sure it ever comes back for any of us unless we make a cognitive effort to understand.

In my first year of dental school, we spent ten hours a week working on the dental anatomy of teeth. We would spend one week per each type of tooth using dental wax to create the perfect tooth by looking at diagrams of the tooth from five different angles. And then we would be graded on it. Some weeks were better than others, but I was an average tooth waxer. I viewed this as a mundane task that would result in ridicule from some instructors, so there was no fun or desire to excel.

Fast forward to ten years after graduation. As I studied with the some of the masters in my profession, the light bulb went off. The shape and contour of teeth determine the health and cleansability of the surrounding area, allow for normal chewing, normal and natural-sounding speech, and proper aesthetics. Wow, if someone had taken five minutes to explain this to me in 1981, dental school might have been a little easier, at least in helping me understand why we were jumping through a lot of hoops and hurdles.

Why is the key. It helps give clarity and direction to what I do in my business. When faced with a proposal from a vendor or a suggestion from my staff, I always ask why first. When I am talking with patients, I explain why we need to do something at the beginning, and deal with what and how and when after. It helps create understanding and buy-in from the patient, which makes my life easier.

Most businesses have vendors who come by offering a special, or we get potential vendors making cold calls trying to get in the door. In the dental world, our dental supply representatives will get a special from a manufacturer and then they go into each office to make the case for this special as being something we can't live without. Recently, my local rep came and said, "Dr. Scott, I have this great material on special I know you are going to love."

My reply was short and sweet, "No I'm not." I looked at her and asked, "*Why* would I try this and change to this product? Did I ask for this information, was I having a problem with what I was using, was there a benefit I was missing out on? *Why* would I change?" After a short silence, the conversation was over because she had no good answer.

The same principle applies to goal setting and initiatives for our business throughout the year. There are lots of great products and materials available for every business, and lots of neat technology. If you bought everything, your business would not be around very long. Ask yourself *why* first, and everything else will fall into place.

> *"People don't buy WHAT you do,*
> *they buy WHY you do it."*
>
> –Simon Sinek

ACTION STEP: Look at things you have recently done, both in your personal and business lives. Ask yourself *why* you did it and see if there is a good answer. Make sure you watch the TED talk video, "Start with Why," and start by using *why* as your first question, not the last one.

LIFE'S TWO BIG PROBLEMS, AND YOURS TOO, IF YOU LET THEM ...

The two biggest issues that cause most of the problems in the world involve:
1. Power
2. Money

If you look around the world, in our current political environment, and in our business lives, very seldom is there anything else that causes us problems. If you can find a way to control these two aspects of your life, you will be in much better shape in every way.

Ego is needed to be successful. Ego propels you to move forward and to believe in all you do. Problems arise when ego gets out of control and becomes a controlling factor instead of a motivating factor.

First, control your ego. That does not mean give up control or ignore your business and management responsibilities. But it does mean pay attention to how you do things. I have had the privilege of meeting many fellow dentists and business owners through the years. The good leaders understand how to control their egos, and the lousy ones just don't get it. Poor leaders think they are more important than anyone else; they aren't open to learning about better ways to do things; they believe their staff doesn't know enough to have a say in what happens in the office or even offer suggestions; and they will have more staff turnover than you can imagine. Why? They feel the need to over-control and over-manage, and they have their priorities in the wrong place. A "my way or the highway" attitude leads to dismissing many good employees, and starting a revolving door of staff members. Many times, a poor leader's priority is focused on money, and their control of it. But in actuality, it's just the opposite. Hire the right people, train them, spend time with them, give them responsibility, value them, hold them accountable, and they will help you reap more success and more profits.

I lovingly refer to my staff as a bunch of rejects. Most of my long-time staff members either left their previous employers because they didn't like working for them, or they were fired for some reason. These wonderful "rejects" have proven to be fantastic, long-time, loyal staff members I would not trade for anyone. They have become superstars who perform at the highest level, are masters at customer relations, and work well with their fellow team members. Treat people fairly and with respect, and you will get the same thing in return, plus a whole lot more.

As dentists or business owners, we have worked hard to get where we are. We could not have done it without powerful egos that made us believe in our goals and our efforts. But how we control those egos is the key.

My staff sometimes refers to me as "Big Daddy," and I love it for two reasons. First, I am a dad in the sense that I take care of them. Sure, I dole out money, but it is more than that. I help them grow and succeed in my office, and hopefully in life, and I reap the benefits of their efforts and they reap the benefits of my genuine care and concern for them. The second reason is that I am the boss. While I give my team responsibilities and control of many aspects of my practice, I am "Big Daddy" in control of everything. I can and will be nurturing, caring, understanding, firm, and flexible as needed. But, I can and will deal with them in a tough, yet compassionate, way when needed. I am clear in my expectations and goals, and I hold them accountable. I am fair and honest and am the kind of boss who is easy to please if you do what I expect and work hard.

So, what kind of leader are you or do you want to be? Are you the controller that fails to get the best out of your staff? Do you supervise using the fear factor, or do you guide and lead by example? Does your staff like you or do they tolerate you for the paycheck? Is it all about you, or is it about your staff and your patients?

> *"If your actions inspire others to
> dream more, learn more, do more, and
> become more, you are a leader."*
> –Simon Sinek, *Leaders Eat Last: Why Some
> Teams Pull Together and Others Don't*

As my wife and I engage with practices in our consulting business, we have yet to see a practice where this power factor is not in play. For staff problems, ego is a much bigger issue than money. Egotists don't want to give up control of their domain, risk the importance of their role in the office, or share the spotlight. But it's not just the staff members with the out-of-control egos. We see many doctors who are unwilling to listen to the great advice and counsel of their staff, and their practice suffers from this.

I can spend days talking about the issue of power and its effects on your practice. Control it, and you will be successful. Fail to control it, and your practice will be a mirage. You may make money and consider yourself successful, but it's just an illusion. And one that will complicate your practice and add hours, days, and years of stress and problems that you could avoid.

Now, let me be clear about money. I work very hard and am rewarded for doing so. We all work to make a living and provide the necessities—and the extras—in life. I provide a wonderful place for my staff to work, compensate them nicely, and spend a lot of extra time managing my practice. And while I must oversee the money and profit from my efforts, money does not control me. I am meticulous in my efforts to watch expenses, manage my cash flow, and create a very well-run practice. I do not penny pinch and drive my staff crazy over this. I buy my dental supplies from a large dental supply company. In today's world, I could have my staff buy everything over the internet and save some money. I could do the same thing with my insurance company. But in the end, I would lose. As a good, loyal customer, I get great service, and having my practice up and running at full speed is crucial.

While I was on vacation a few years ago, my partner called to tell me we had a water leak that had backed up into our compressor, and we now had water in our air lines. Understand that water and air do not mix well in the dental environment. Puddles of water had leaked into the walls, and we had a full-blown disaster on our hands. My dental supply company arrived at my office immediately. The branch manager was there as well to make sure they took care of this disaster appropriately. Our insurance representative was there immediately as well, and they were all at the office over the weekend to oversee the repairs. They coordinated their services to address the problems and had us up and running within hours, not days or weeks. They coordinated the replacement of over $25,000 in ruined equipment, and their entire team was available 24/7. The extra money I spend with them is well worth it, and gives me the peace of mind to focus my efforts on dentistry, and not get bogged down worrying about saving a few dollars here and there.

Ultimately, my choice of companies is really about the relationship we have. Can you get the same supplies from the large mail-order supply companies? Sure. But I would rather invest more money with the right people and get a better result for my office and my patients. I am rewarded with less stress and a well-coordinated outcome. Some may consider this a waste of money; I consider it a blessing. When I leave at the end of the day, my outside life begins, and I can sleep well at night and enjoy the good life with my wife, children, and friends. I consider this peace of mind worth the extra money.

If you have ever been involved with any practice or business, ninety-nine percent of all personnel problems involve power or money. It's as simple as that. When a staff feels unappreciated and threatened, then they are grossly underpaid and overworked, at least in their minds, and it will never be enough. Someone else is making more than them. A friend in another office is getting this perk and they aren't. The solution to this problem is to make them feel appreciated, thank them for all they do, and acknowledge what a great job they did, so money as an issue is off the table. In many cases, people may love the job or business they work in, they just don't feel their boss appreciates what they do.

My staff doesn't bicker about money. I pay them well, but also make sure there is room to grow. I provide lots of perks; some cost me a reasonable amount of money and some cost very little. I thank them a lot for making our practice successful and for taking good care of our patients. If it weren't for my staff, I wouldn't be doing as well as I am. So, sharing my success with them is important for my staff, but it is more important for me. Let me stress that the key qualities I give them are value and appreciation. It costs me little and returns huge benefits.

Do not confuse being a good steward of your money with being cheap. "Cheap" is not providing your staff with proper tools and supplies, using cheap labs that give you and your patients sub-par restorations, not spending money to fix things, having an office that is fifteen years out of date, reusing things you should not reuse, and the list can go on. Be fair to your staff and they will be fair to you.

A story that sums this all up:

My sons played competitive soccer on the highest club level while teenagers, and a team from England came to town for a week to compete in tournaments and friendly matches. It was a great opportunity for everyone to forge new friendships and invaluable experiences. In the spring of 2010, a volcanic eruption in Iceland grounded flights to and from Europe for over two weeks. The English team was stranded, with no way to get home and no more money. A quick email to our local soccer club and a few stories in the newspaper brought an amazing response. Over 300 families responded with monetary donations and tickets to amusement parks and golf tournaments. A professional football player donated $5,000. He didn't know any of these kids. I wrote a check (not as big as that one) because I hope people would help my sons if they were in the same situation. Needless to say, the players' two-week additional time in Charlotte was a life-changing event, both for them and for our community.

In the coach's thanks for the outpouring of support and kindness, he shared a story he had learned earlier in his life from one of his own coaches and mentors. The moral of the story was: It is nice to be important, but it is much more important to be nice. This sums things up very well.

Be nice to your staff and make them feel important. Thank them for their efforts and support. Eliminate the ego and power plays that can and do go on. And finally, spend more time making staff and patients feel appreciated, and you will get more than you could ever imagine in return.

My staff appreciates how I treat them and how much I value their efforts. I do work hard at it, but it also comes pretty naturally to me. I like being nice. And trust me, my staff likes me this way a whole lot better than when I get upset or disappointed in them.

We all like to feel important, but it is a whole lot more important to my success in work and life to be nice.

> **ACTION STEP:** Review your relationships with your staff and the people around you, especially as they relate to power and money. Give it serious and truthful consideration. Make a list. Break it into positive and negative items. Pick three key areas you want to correct, and three areas in which you want to accentuate the good you are doing. With a focused effort, it will not take long to use power, ego, and money to your advantage.

Taking care of problems is a sign of strength and commitment to your staff. Be nice and in control of yourself, and your staff will not be disappointed in you.

VISION

To put it simply, it all begins with a vision. Vision is the future. Vision is where you want to go. I'm not talking about the vision to be a dentist and have a practice and treat patients. I'm talking about having a vision for the *type* of practice and business you want to have, and *how* you want it to operate. This is your vision for your staff, your office environment, your marketing, and your daily operations. If you have a vision, is it in writing? Does your staff know what it is? Does your partner know? If you are like me many years ago, I doubt it. It's not something that we are trained to do, or something we normally talk about.

KEY TAKEAWAY: You must spend time working on your business, not just working in it. We are so in tune to the technical aspects of our practices that we spend little time on the crucial pieces that will make things more efficient and more profitable.

Creating a vision takes time and thought. It takes a plan to put your vision in place. And, it takes a constant effort to revisit it, adapt it to the current environment, and add to it. It took me a long time before I fully understood this idea, but once I did, it has given me direction and purpose, which are two things I could not do without, and neither can you. Yes, you can muddle through things and be reasonably successful without a vision, but you will ultimately fail to get to the end. And that is the key.

Years ago, a friend showed me the cover of a music album. This was in the old days, when music was on vinyl records and the covers usually had some amazing artwork on the front. On the cover of this particular album was a picture of a guy staring off the back of a caboose looking down the tracks, with the caption "Starting at the End." I think of this often. You can't be sure where you're going if you don't know where you want to end up.

What is your vision for the "End"?

I'm not talking about when you want to retire and how much money you want to have. We can leave that to your financial planner and their fancy retirement calculators that give you more info than you can digest. What I'm talking about is what you want your business to look like, feel like, what kind of staff you want to have, how you want it to operate, etc.

Whether you are in business for a year, fifteen years, or thirty years, having a picture or vision of the end will determine everything. Now I'm not suggesting that someone just out of school or a few years into the working world will know exactly what the end will look like, but I am suggesting that looking to the future will determine how successful you will be in reaching your goals.

My quick story—I was an associate for ten months at a business that failed, then held another associate position for eighteen months. I then bought in as a junior partner for two years (tough time), and finally bought out the senior partner after less than five years in practice. I turned this into a very successful and profitable practice, but I was practicing just to keep up. No vision, no goals, just handling everything on the fly. My patients were scheduled for their preventive visits eight months out instead of six months because we were booked solid with no end in sight. We were all running from chair to chair and patient to patient.

My success was swallowing me whole each and every day. Until … I developed a vision for SmileCharlotte. My vision was to bring in an associate and hopefully a partner for the long-term, create a new and thriving structure for myself, my staff, and my patients, and to create a practice of loyal patients and caring staff. I knew what I wanted to accomplish. The next step was to get my staff on board. I spent a lot of time talking to my staff and getting them "on the train." I spelled out my vision and put it in writing, told them what would be expected of them, and asked for their buy-in. For me, they were either in completely or, as I told them quite clearly, I would throw them off the train if they didn't go by themselves. No dragging feet, no complaining or blaming others. This was a large undertaking and it had to be a team effort. I couldn't do it without them. But they needed to understand and embrace one thing —the vision of where we were going.

> *"Faith in the endgame helps you live through the months or years of buildup."*
> –Jim Collins, Good to Great

KEY TAKEAWAY: Give yourself and your employees a vision and a path they understand. It can and will help them understand what you expect from them. Be honest about your expectations and what you want, but also be realistic. Give them training and direction and most importantly, your support. If they still don't get it, help them find another place to work. This isn't being mean; it's just being a responsible leader who holds people accountable.

The Vision Process

If you are looking for a cookie-cutter template, there is none. The process of creating a vision for your business is as unique as you are. A vision is about seeing beyond what's in front of you at the moment. You can't quite touch it or feel it, but you know it's there somewhere. Some questions to consider:

- What kind of practice (or business) do you have? Solo, partnership, associateship?
- What kind of dentistry (or other work) do you want to do?
- What types of treatments do you want to add in the future?
- What are your skills? What should you not do? What will you refer?
- How do you want to offer your services?
- What kind of dentist (or … you fill in the blank) do you want to be?
- What technologies do you want to add to your practice?
- What kinds of systems and procedures do you want to have in place?
- What kind of boss do you want to be?
- What kinds of business practices will you use?
- How will you train your team?
- What are your expectations of them?

> **KEY TAKEAWAY:** Business success is a marathon, not a sprint. If you go too fast in the beginning, you'll burn out before you reach the end. Having a clear vision will keep you on the right path.

As you start to ponder these things, I want you to think about Walt Disney. We all know what kind of place he created, and it all started with a movie. But it wasn't just about the movie. Walt Disney's secret was creating one thing—memories.

Walt Disney got it. He wanted something special that would leave a lasting impression on his guests. Everything he did was tied into his vision. No cutting corners that would affect the final product. All employees were trained in the Disney way. No products were allowed that did not reflect the quality and special nature of the Disney name. Disney's success, then and now, is the unwavering commitment to creating memories. Those memories are revisited year after year by the same people doing the same thing and paying their hard-earned money for the same wonderful feeling. Walt Disney had a vision for himself and his company, and it continues today, long after his death.

We, in dentistry or any other business, are no different from Walt Disney, except for one thing. Most of us don't have a vision for what we want our business to be. We have a set of wonderful skills and think that's all we need. It can work for a while, but in the long run, you run out of energy and direction, and you lose the ability to sustain your success.

> *Vision is about having your eyes wide open.*

Find some real quiet time, away from the office. Start with a blank piece of paper. Write down your thoughts and ideas with no preconceived plan. Don't look to modify what you're already doing, but rather look at it as starting from scratch and trying to build your business so it is memorable and sustainable. Write your vision down and share it with family, friends, partners, key employees, etc. Rework and modify as you see fit.

Share your vision with your staff, and have an open and honest discussion. Help them understand the direction you want to take your office in the future, and ask them to join you on this journey. Post it in your office so you see it every day. Post on your website and share with your patients. It will be contagious and will help guide you on your path to success and fulfillment. It will become your guiding principle, helping you move forward year after year.

ACTION STEP: What are people saying about your brand? Be honest! Create a vision statement for your practice. Involve your staff in this process. It can and will be very powerful for determining who is on your train for the long haul and creating a cohesive team. For my vision statement, check out my website under "Our Team" at www.smilecharlotte.com.

GOALS

While *vision* is about the future, *goals* are about today. Goals get you to move forward with a clear plan of action and keep your business true to your vision. I was always told to set goals, and good things would come. Only problem is, that whole process seemed like a bunch of useless work that would get me nowhere. There was a clear disconnect between the work necessary for the process, and the benefits of the outcome. It may have taken a long time for me to get it, but setting goals has been the most energizing and practice-changing process of my business life. And if you will begin this process for yourself and your business, I guarantee you'll see clear, measurable results.

Here is my story about goal setting. I was the anti-goal setting guy. I could not understand how or why you would waste your time on this process. All the great books written on this subject were worthless in my mind. I spent a week with Zig Ziglar at his leadership and goal-setting workshop in the late 1980s, and I was going to use that information to be the leader for our office's monthly two-hour learning sessions. Well, we started out strong, and this lasted for a few months, and then completely died out in less than six months. Our learning sessions died for two reasons: 1) both the staff and I did not understand the goal-setting process and, 2) it was boring and not very engaging (at least at that time) for all parties involved. I really didn't believe or understand how this could positively impact my office and my team.

When it was time to implement my vision for SmileCharlotte, my dental practice, I realized that I needed structure. And goal-setting was the answer. Since 2000, my office has used the first Friday in January for a full-day goal-setting session, and it's one of the most dynamic and impactful things we do all year. It's something my staff looks forward to and a tremendous buy-in for teamwork and energy. Our goal-setting day takes a lot of preliminary work to be effective, and we spend a lot of time getting ready for this day. We clearly want it to be impactful, but we also want it to be fun.

Be strategic in your thinking as you plan your goals. Ask yourself, "How will these goals benefit my practice or business?" Something may benefit your staff, you, or the customers, but there has to be a clearly defined benefit, or what seems like a reasonable goal can easily become a distraction.

Goal setting is about these five key components:
1. Purpose
2. Actions
3. Measures
4. Accountability
5. Adaptability

Let me emphasize the importance of these five key components. Use them when setting goals. It will help ensure the process works effectively and efficiently. It doesn't automatically mean you will reach your goal as expected; it may mean you need to find a different way there. And isn't that what life is all about?

Purpose

Setting goals just for the heck of it or because someone told you to do it just plain foolish. Yet we do it all the time. There must be a method to your madness, or you will either go mad or drive everyone around you crazy.

Every goal must have a purpose. And, again, the first question you need to answer is "Why?" Purpose will provide clarity. It will save you money, time, and aggravation.

In dentistry, we listen to some guru talk about a product or technology at a seminar or read it in a journal and think we need to buy it for our practice. Got to have it and can't live without it. So when someone says we should all have an intraoral camera in our practice, is it a good idea or a bad idea? It all depends on your practice. But what did I do in the early 1990s when intraoral cameras came out? I bought one. Not sure why, but everyone said you should have it and I thought it could be useful. With no real plan in place or realistic expectation on how to utilize this technology, I basically wasted a lot of money on my first intraoral camera system purchase. And these were not the wireless ones of today. I had rooms hardwired so we could use this very expensive camera. It was too cumbersome to effectively move from room to room, took too much time to hook up and connect to the monitors, and it was such a drag for my staff that they quit on it before I did. Advances in technology have made it easy to use intraoral cameras today, but a clearly defined goal-setting plan is still crucial to implementing this technology into a daily office routine.

Actions

Actions are needed to move your goal forward and reach it. Action involves evaluating the goal to define what steps are needed to make things successful, identifying and what obstacles and limitations may stand in your way. You must include your staff in this process since they are a critical part of almost everything that goes on in your business.

Measures

The only way to know if you have been successful in reaching your goal is to set a measurable component to it. Just saying you are going to do something and expecting it to happen without knowing your end goal will result in failure. These metrics must be monitored regularly and discussed at weekly and monthly meetings. The tendency is for great success at the beginning of any change, but the effort to maintain momentum can and will wane. Tracking your successes and failures is crucial.

Accountability

So, who is responsible for making your goals happen? Is it you, your office manager, or a staff member? Does your staff understand what is expected of them, *and* do they know they will be held accountable for their part in reaching the goal? Ninety-nine percent of the time the answer is "no," and it is clearly the boss's fault for that. It will dramatically increase your success when people know they will be held to a higher standard than just doing the minimum.

Adaptability

It would be great if everything always went according to plan, but that's not going to happen. If you set your goals properly, things will be more predictable. But, in many cases, you need to adapt your goals to ensure you're successful, especially when there's a kink in the system. Adaptability is about being flexible. Making changes can help increase your success. It may even make it easier to reach, and possibly exceed, your goals.

> *What gets written gets measured.*
> *What gets measured gets worked on.*
> *What gets worked on gets better.*

After our annual office goal-setting day, my practice administrator creates a spreadsheet of each goal, and a completion date where indicated, that allows us to monitor, measure, and analyze how we are doing. By writing things down, we are forced to be more accountable throughout the year as we review these goals. We monitor our progress throughout the year, and refer to our goals often. We reach most goals, some we don't, and others we adapt to changing circumstances and decisions.

KEY TAKEAWAY: Setting goals does not have to be complicated and take forever, but you must utilize the five key components if you want to reach your goals. And remember, some goals may not have been a good idea in the first place, and being adaptable and recognizing this is a huge success.

Sometimes, even after going through this process, things will not go as planned. But through your Measures and Adaptability charting, you can change your actions for your benefit. Here is one example from my office. We implemented a new oral cancer screening in addition to our standard screening at each hygiene and new patient visit. With the input of my hygienists, we had a discussion after twelve months to evaluate the status of this service in our office. We found that this new screening was not producing the benefits we thought we would see, which was to find more early signs of tissue changes in the mouth before they became noticeable and more advanced. We found there was no discernable difference between our old process and the new one. We made the decision to stop doing this new screening. Note that this negatively impacted revenues for our hygienists, but it wasn't about money; it was that this didn't meet our goal for the procedure, so we eliminated it from our protocol.

The first thing I do as a consultant with my clients is a vision and goal-setting session. It usually takes four hours to review statistics, talk about opportunities, review problem areas, and talk about ways to move their practice forward and create more profitability. We then create a master plan that we use to make dynamic strategic changes in their business, and then work with their staff to get buy-in. By doing this same thing for your business, as well as your personal life, you will have a clear path for success.

ACTION STEP: Begin to plan for a goal-setting day with your entire team. Your first step may be doing your own goal-setting session by yourself. Then share it with key staff members, and lastly, your entire team.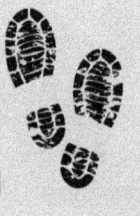

WHO ARE YOU RUNNING WITH?

It is a great big world out there. And no matter how good we are or think we are, we don't have all the answers. Ego has a terrible way of getting in the way of success. We think we have all the answers, we think we can do everything our way, and we corrupt the people we work with by stifling their creativity and input. And we don't like to admit we don't have all the answers. The world is not an island, but a great expanse with so many people to help us, nurture us, and guide us. The key is to open our minds to everything and everyone around us.

The best step you can take to open your mind is to have a mentor or better yet, mentors. People to listen to, people whose examples you can follow, and people to appreciate for their successes. And people to tell you the truth.

For years, my identical twin brother, Steve, and I went for a run every morning. Since my office opens at seven every morning, we met at 5 o'clock for our runs. That may seem a little crazy, but at that hour it's dark, the streets are quiet, the temperature is a little cooler during the hot Charlotte summers, the day has just begun, and the distractions are not there yet. And while Steve and I catch up on family and world affairs, it's also a time to pick each other's brains for ideas and advice. Steve is a CPA and has a keen business sense, and he helps keep me grounded. I do the same for him. Steve has been a mentor for years and probably doesn't know it. So while you don't literally have to run with your mentor, I do and it's great for me. And it's also great to spend time with my brother and best friend.

> **KEY TAKEAWAY:** Mentors don't have to work in your field. But they must be people who are successful, people you respect, and people who have worked hard to get where they are today. Mentors will help give you insight and new perspectives. They will encourage you and ground you. Most of all, they will help you succeed.

Let me give you examples of my mentors so you can appreciate how they have had a tremendous positive impact on my life and practice.

Mentor 1 is Bob Salvin. Bob's short story—he used to sell burs and specialty instruments from the trunk of his car. His car office eventually grew to be an office in his home. He then developed this small home business into an international company, Salvin Dental. His vision for Salvin Dental was, and today still is, "Everything for your Implant Practice but the Implants." Salvin Dental is now in a 40,000-square-foot office/warehouse selling specialty implant supplies and equipment around the world, with customer service and loyalty as the company's number one priority. I have been a part of Bob's dental career as he has been a part of mine. (He has been a patient since I started practicing in 1985 and he helped me find my first associateship coming out of school.) Bob and I share stories, we share books, and he is there for me any time I need him. He has surrounded himself with some incredible people, and it's a joy to talk with Bob and his entire team. Check out Bob's company at www.salvin.com.

Mentor 2 is Jeffrey Gitomer. Jeffrey's short story—he spent most of his career in sales, until he realized there was a better way to sell and to train people. Jeffrey wrote the number one sales book of all time, *The Little Red Book of Sales*, along with over twenty books on topics from customer loyalty to trust to having a "yes" attitude. Jeffrey speaks around the world to numerous major corporations about sales and customer loyalty, and has created a tremendous online presence. I have talked about patient loyalty for years, and Jeffrey and I share a kindred philosophy about treating people the right way and how to sell dentistry. Jeffrey is brutally honest, makes suggestions to me about anything and everything, and, most importantly, also acknowledges the great stuff we do and how we provide great care. We talk about life, dentistry (he's another long-time patient), and success. Check out Jeffrey's company at www.gitomer.com.

Live your life like an octopus.

I describe this idea of mentorship to my three sons as the "tentacles." The longer the reach, the more contacts you develop, and the more information you can learn, the more successful you will be. The cliché we have all heard is, "It's not what you know, but who you know." Never have truer words been spoken.

My son Nate went to China for two months during the summer of 2009 for an internship through the University of North Carolina. Part of this involved working for a company in Beijing while also doing some class work. While the school would find the students a place to work, students were encouraged to find something on their own if they could. I contacted a good friend of mine in Charlotte who had a connection to an orthopedist who had a company in Beijing. After a few phone calls and a telephone interview, Nate had an internship in China. But more importantly, he learned a powerful lesson about the "tentacles" and extending your reach, because you never know where it may lead you.

"One of the greatest values of mentors is the ability to see ahead what others cannot see and to help them navigate a course to their destination."

–John C. Maxwell

KEY TAKEAWAY: Don't recreate the wheel. Learn from others no matter what business they are in. Good, solid, successful business practices cross all boundaries and carry through to almost everything we do. Ask someone how they do things or what they would suggest to handle a difficult situation. Meet with your mentors regularly. The agenda is not crucial, but the gathering of knowledge is priceless.

I have lots of mentors, some with bigger roles than others. Surround yourself with successful, driven people, and you will rev your engine and work a lot smarter and harder. During our annual goal-setting and throughout the year, I have had some of these mentors speak with my team. It is a powerful way to impact my staff as well as my business.

ACTION STEP: In the next month, meet with three people you respect and want to learn more about. Ask about their successes and failures, their motivations, or whatever moves you. Make notes after your meeting and create a folder (preferably on your computer) for Mentor Knowledge. Find ways to integrate some of the ideas gleaned from your mentors into your practice. Then continue to cultivate mentors across all fields who will help you grow and reach your goals. Remember, good ideas and processes are not always field-specific. What works in law, banking, accounting, technology, or sales professions can and will work in dentistry—or vice versa.

LOYALTY: YOUR OWN PERSONAL MULTI-LEVEL MARKETING PROGRAM

I have always been intrigued by the idea of loyalty. With so many choices in this world, why do people continue to return to the same places and businesses?

Loyalty is defined as "a strong feeling of support and allegiance."

The key word here is "feeling." Loyalty is an emotion. It is created by a person, business, team, etc., that builds a deep sense of commitment based on how you feel.

In my business, I was always fascinated by why my customers/patients come back to see us year after year; why others leave; and why some come, leave, and then come back. And the bottom line is that it all comes down to whether you have created a loyal patient or not.

Patients only know one thing about us: Do they like us? They don't know if we do great work. Everything is great if we don't hurt them and things look good. It's that simple. Now let me be clear that doing less than excellent work is unacceptable. But patients don't have a clue if our crowns and fillings fit well and were done correctly. They *do* know if they like me, if I didn't hurt them (or I seemed to care if I did), and if the services that I provide look and feel okay.

As I have thought about why patients are loyal, I thought of all the people and places I am loyal to. From restaurants to doctors, stores, friends, etc., I thought of why I returned year after year and gave my hard-earned money to certain people and places of business, and my time to my friends. And the key to this is a sense of loyalty and how they made me feel. I felt appreciated and welcome and valued.

> **KEY TAKEAWAY:** Loyalty is a key to success. It is the pot of gold at the end of the rainbow. It is the gold medal of patient and staff relations. And just so I am really clear, *loyalty* is the key to your business success.

Over the years, we have all had some interaction with a multi-level marketing company, from those selling cleaning supplies to those selling vitamins, healthcare products, nutritional products, etc. In a nutshell, the company rewards consumers for buying their products and then selling them to others. This continues with multiple levels of sellers with different compensation levels. It is all built on a pyramid shape that depends on all people at all levels being engaged and active. In the end, the more salespeople are involved, the more money the company makes.

What if you could create your own multi-level marketing company in your business? And what if it were one where you had people buying products and services year after year, and they referred others to your practice. This is what loyalty will do for you; it creates your very own marketing campaign. And the best part is you get to keep all the profits. Let me be clear. You get to keep *all* the profits, not just a portion of them like all the schemes out there sold as passive income. Stick with what you know and what you have spent many years invested in—dentistry. And this way, you don't have to share the rewards of your hard work.

Loyalty is when people will drive from anywhere to see you, refer their friends and co-workers to see you, and follow your recommendations without question. Loyalty is earned. The two key groups that must be loyal to your practice for long-term success are your patients and your staff. You must have both.

Staff loyalty is the easiest way to make your life easy. Treat people with respect, talk to them and train them, care for them, respect them, and show your appreciation for how much they help you. I have worked hard to develop a loyal staff. Many of them worked in other offices for years, some changing jobs every few years as they grew weary of where they worked, or they were fired, or they were unhappy with their jobs. They needed a change, and I was the change they needed. I have almost no staff turnover. They come and they stay, unless I ask them to leave. I am demanding, and people like to work hard if they know their efforts are appreciated. I tell my staff that if they think there is something better, go find it. No one takes me up on this offer. I pay them well, but not over the top. I show respect for their skills, value their efforts, and treat them as family, and I thank them often. In return, I never worry about my staff. We have a great time at work, even when we work hard, and we have a great time playing when we play.

> **KEY TAKEAWAY:** Loyalty begins with your staff, because they will not be loyal unless they feel appreciated and valued. If your staff isn't feeling special, then you are already losing ground before you start. If your staff members feel appreciated and valued, they will treat your patients the same way.

Patient loyalty is the Utopia of practice goals. Get a practice full of loyal patients, and the revenues will continue for years to come. How do you get patients to be loyal and not come to see you just based on your fees or the insurance plans you participate in? Here are some of the key qualities of a loyal practice:

1. Friendly
2. Caring
3. Concerned
4. Make patients feel valued and appreciated
5. Respect
6. Feels like family
7. Attention to detail
8. Follow-through
9. Excellent care
10. Nice environment

You can probably add ten more qualities, and I suggest you do, but this should give you the basis from which to improve your practice by concentrating on these areas to grow your loyalty base.

Let me tell you about Tim. I have seen Tim as a patient for over thirty years, and he is a great guy who comes to see me three times a year. When Tim needs work, he never questions my suggestions or asks for another option. He knows I am recommending what I would do for myself, and that's what he wants. The neatest part about Tim is that he comes to see me from Hong Kong, where he lives most of the year. Yes, he visits Charlotte on a regular basis, but he goes nowhere else for his dental care. Tim is loyal to me and we would do anything for him.

Let me tell you about David. David is a friend and business associate. He and his wife and two children have been in my practice for over eighteen years.

Think about the residual income year after year that I get from their return visits for regular preventive care, and the added bonus and profits from treatment and elective procedures they may need. This family (and tons more just like them) returns year after year, and this is money in the bank for me.

It is much easier to fish in a pond where you know the fish have been biting.

It is much easier to keep a loyal patient than to spend money on marketing in an attempt to find new patients through the internet, direct campaigns, or other programs. Make sure your patients are happy, treated well, and appreciated, and they will be loyal to your practice for years to come.

> **KEY TAKEAWAY:** Loyalty is about repeat income and patient referrals. Understand how this significantly impacts your practice, and you will frame your actions to nurture loyalty in your staff, your patients, and most importantly, yourself.

ACTION STEP: Take fifteen minutes and write down five businesses that you go to repeatedly. Ask yourself why you do that, how often you return, and how much you spend there. Most importantly, understand the qualities and feelings these businesses illicit in you, and then duplicate those feelings in your business.

HOW

Whether you are in a big town with hundreds or maybe thousands of dentists, or in a small town with a handful of dentists, there is very little that defines or separates you from the "competition." And while it may be a friendly competition where we don't undercut on price or whatever, it is still a competition to get people in your door and not someone else's. There is only one thing that separates you from any other dentist, and that's *how*. How you do things, how you treat patients, and how you operate your office is the key. It is all about *how!*

While my wife was reading one of those airline magazines on a long flight, there was an excerpt from the book *How: Why How We Do Anything Means Everything* by Dov Seidman. In this excerpt, he stressed the importance of how we do things as the key to success. One simple word—how. The idea of *how* we do things correctly or incorrectly is not exclusive to anyone.

Jack Welch, one of the great business minds who led General Electric for decades, said the main reason for his company's success was *how* GE did things. He wasn't worried about his competitors knowing about his products or his company, because he knew GE's advantage was in how they did things, how his sales and productions teams went about their business, and how they took care of their customers. No one else was as invested as GE in managing *how* they did things, and it showed in their profitability and success for years.

During one of our office goal-setting sessions, we spent some time working on the topic of new patient acquisition. The key question we posed was how to increase our internal referrals. With the idea of *how* as the focus, we were able to define specific things we could do. We were already doing some things, but we weren't being effective or rigorous in how we did them. The fun part of this exercise is that we gave our staff some video cameras to record the good and not-so-good approaches we were using (incredibly funny and a great time) instead of writing them down and giving a report. It was a great way to role play and make some simple, easy suggestions to all staff (doctors included) on *how* to ask for referrals in a simple, non-confrontational way. The added benefit of this exercise was getting everyone involved. And while we didn't find any Academy Award winners, it was a hysterical, yet very engaging lesson to see people acting out their ideas.

> **KEY TAKEAWAY:** When (not if) you need to take action or make some improvement to your practice, remember to ask "How?" and it will propel you in the right direction.
> And keep asking "How" questions on a continual basis.

The greatest benefit was the idea to make 2010 our year of PLAY, our Patient Loyalty Appreciation Year. This was a year-long campaign to thank our patients for their loyalty, ask for referrals from them, and reward them for their referrals with monthly giveaways and a grand prize of $1,200 in free dentistry. We also had a party for our patients by celebrating my twenty-fifth year in practice. Over 300 people showed up for free food, free drinks, and music in our office parking lot. We wore buttons that said "Free Dentistry? Ask Me!" which served to start the conversation in a friendly and easy manner for all our staff. We changed *how* we asked for new patient referrals, and it proved to be very successful for us.

ACTION STEP: Spend some time answering these questions—How does my office operate? How do my patients view my office? How efficient and effective is my staff? How well do we treat our patients? How do I communicate with my staff and patients? Add some of your own questions, but by answering these questions honestly, you'll find the areas that still need work to improve your operations and profits. When confounded by a problem area, ask the question "How?" as the starting point to solving your problem.

NUMBERS DON'T LIE

People may lie about numbers (just ask Bernie Madoff and other white-collar criminals), but the numbers themselves do not lie. Statistics are used each and every day to prove this point or to refute that idea. Averages, means, medians, standard deviations, and comparisons of numbers are a way of life. Yet no one really puts numbers in the context of how to use them. In school, we were told to track certain numbers or were given averages to measure our practice's success.

For years, I read journals that gave us percentages for overhead and other specific areas such as staff salaries, rent, supplies, etc. And I tracked these statistics and wrote them down and referred back to them all the time. Okay, maybe not all the time; how about *regularly?* (Or maybe just once a year to see how they compared to last year.) You get my point, which is that most people don't track their practice numbers. And more to my point, they don't track the right numbers or use this information correctly.

The number one reason to track your statistics is to help improve your performance and help you adapt your operations, not just to say you did. Two of the keys to reaching your goals are monitoring your goals and adapting to the changing environment, and the numbers you track determine whether you are operating successfully or need to modify your operations.

Numbers don't lie; people do.

Many years ago, when I was considering the purchase of a practice, I got some great advice from a long-time accountant who was also my brother's boss at the time. I sat down with him with stacks of financial reports and spreadsheets and he asked me one question over and over, "Are the numbers good?" I answered "yes" because I had them in front of me, but he kept repeating the question, "Are the numbers good?" So, to answer his question, I went home and spent the weekend really delving into the reports. I found the numbers were *not* good, and the business was *not* worth what I was being told. I still purchased the business, but it was at a much better and more accurate price. I repeated this same scenario in 2013 as our practice purchased a retiring dentist's practice. I spent considerable time evaluating the numbers, the schedule, and the background information, and was able to obtain the practice at a truer and much lower price than was being asked.

Tracking numbers just to do it is a waste of time. You must use this information to your advantage, and it's easy to do. And it's empowering as you share these numbers with your staff. After all, we couldn't do it without them. You should identify key areas of your operations, and areas that drive your profit engine. Set goals for these key statistics, track them on a monthly basis (you can do it daily but don't drive yourself too crazy), compare them to previous numbers and to your goal, and either reward yourself for a job well done or alter your operations to meet your goals.

Example: We track lost hygiene production. In a nutshell, we determine how many open units (ten-minute increments) each hygienist has based on cancellations not filled, broken appointments, and/or inefficient scheduling. We then multiply that by our basic hygiene fee, which is the total of our cleaning and exam fees. It gives us a reasonably good number for lost production that we will never get back. Remember, you can't go back in time. We may see that patient in the future, but we never get that lost time back. By tracking this number for years, I know our lost production is around five to eight percent a month. And when our lost production goes up, I ask "Why and How" did this happen. Was there something we did wrong, did we fail to really work the schedule to fill cancellations, or did we just have a bad month for no-shows? It allows us to consistently track our performance. My hygiene coordinator understands what this number should be, and she usually receives lots of positive feedback from me for her efforts to keep this within our average range.

> **KEY TAKEAWAY:** Numbers are the only way to monitor your success and hold people accountable. The worst thing you can do is track numbers and do nothing with them. The best business managers are the ones who can process these numbers and put them to use in a productive and profitable way.

Develop your own key statistics; the ones you feel are important to your office. Put them in a spreadsheet and track them daily, monthly, and yearly. Share them with your entire office and let them do ninety-nine percent of the tracking. And if you have an office manager who does this for you, look at the statistics. Remember, they don't lie.

WHO'S DRIVING YOUR TRAIN?

The most important function of a CEO is to provide a clear, detailed path for their business. They must understand and explain the goals and direction of the office, detail systems and performance that will drive the operations, train and evaluate staff, monitor performance, modify operations as needed, etc., etc., etc. And if that's not enough, dentists must do this while being the main revenue producer. I bet most people don't realize the complexity of running a business in general, let alone a dental practice where the CEO is on the frontline, not in an office.

I call this the "train." The train can have many cars, carry different loads, make lots of pick-ups and drop-offs along the way, and collect fees for services rendered. And success is based on one thing—getting everyone on the train to pull in the same direction. The doctor is the engineer, the conductor, the guy stoking the fire, and the person putting fires out if necessary. While this may seem overwhelming, these duties are eased by the staff we employ.

KEY TAKEAWAY: Get great people on your train.

You may be able to squeeze a good staff person on your train, but you must have great ones to keep the train moving steadily and swiftly forward. If you have some not-so-good staff members who cannot or will not function how you need them to, tell them to get off your train. It is *your* train, not theirs. The biggest mistake most businesses make is hanging on to a bad employee too long. They will kill your office environment, drive your other staff crazy, and you can't imagine what they are doing to your patients. Did I mention they are costing you money and probably giving you some sleepless nights? One of the benefits of a great staff is they will usually help you get rid of this person because a bad staffer is a drag on them as well as you.

Years ago, as I embarked on adding an associate, I met with my existing staff. I had to explain myself, the changes that were about to come, and how we would handle this. I talked about hiring three new staff members in addition to the new associate dentist, and the magnitude of the positive changes that were to come. And in the simplest of terms, I invited them to join me on the train. I needed them to help pull the train forward and make it go smoothly and effectively. I invited them to join me on this new, exciting, and scary journey. But I told them they could not and would not slow my train down. No dragging of feet or lack of energy would be tolerated. We would not survive if this happened. I asked each one if they wanted to be on the train or not. If not, no hard feelings and I would help find them a job that would better serve them.

In the book, *Good to Great* by Jim Collins, he mentions that one of the biggest keys to a company's or business's success is getting the right people working for you. Mediocre people will get you mediocre results no matter what you do. Once you have the right people on board, you can train them, create expectations of them, and give them the freedom to succeed.

> *"Letting the wrong people hang around is unfair to all the right people, as they inevitably find themselves compensating for the inadequacies of the wrong people."*
> —James C. Collins, Good to Great

KEY TAKEAWAY: Spend some time thinking about your train, your practice. What direction is it going, does your staff understand where you are headed and what is expected of them, and most importantly, do you have the right people on your train? And you must convey and teach them to do things the right way instead of just letting them do it their way. Are you investing the time and energy to master the role you must play to run an effective business? Set goals to make sure your train is heading where you want it to, and make sure no one is dragging you down, including yourself. Invest time each week managing your practice and your staff.

Let's talk about the role of the CEO in a small business (a dental office in my case). They must fill all of the following roles and then some:
1. Chief Executive Officer
2. Chief Engaging Officer
3. Chief Enforcement Officer
4. Chief Encouragement Officer
5. Chief Enlightenment Officer
6. Add your own CEO description

You cannot overstate the role of the dentist in their practice. The key is to view your practice as a business that just so happens to provide dental services. If you forget about the business part of your practice, you will leave lots of money in the pockets of others. You must spend time working *on* your practice instead of just *in* it. Running a business takes time and effort, and trying to squeeze it all in between patients and during lunch is not practical, effective, or useful. You have made a huge monetary investment in your practice/business and in turn, you must invest time in it so it runs like it should.

> **ACTION STEP:** Read books on leadership and business principles. Ask for help if needed. Contact professionals and consultants who can help you identify and master the skills you need to be an effective CEO. Your mentors can help with this as well.

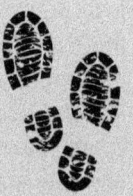

KNOWLEDGE AND INNOVATION

Remember your days in school, where you couldn't wait for the day to end? And this was at 7:30 a.m., just as you started your day. It didn't end there. The weekend couldn't come fast enough, teacher work days were too few and far between, fall and spring breaks seemed years away, and summer break was never long enough. I still yearn for those days when I could get two months off. Only problem now is that I haven't found anyone to support me while my income drops to zero. So I keep working hard to provide for my office and my family.

What prevents us all from getting burned out and getting bogged down in the mundane responsibilities of work? The answer is knowledge. Knowledge comes in many forms, but the concept of learning and bettering ourselves can and should be the stimulus that motivates us to set our goals high and strive to reach them.

I love to talk with college students and recent graduates and share my years of wisdom and experiences with them. I look them in the eye and tell them I am going to give them the best advice they will ever hear. They look intently and seriously at me, and then I say ...

*"You Don't Know S#*T."*

They have not had any real experiences to gain true knowledge. As dental students just coming out of school, they have been taught procedures and services, all under the direction and control of a professor. Same for any profession. New graduates have knowledge, but they have no clue how to truly use this knowledge in the real world. My reason for saying this is to stress the importance of becoming life-long learners, something that turns us into seasoned professionals. My first year of work was so very different from the fifth, or the tenth, or the twentieth. And even today, after over thirty years in practice, I'm still learning.

Think about what you would be doing if things never changed or the world around us never changed. Obviously, each day is different from the previous one, and knowledge is the reason.

I had a conversation with my college-age son's friend. We were talking about his college days, what he was studying, and his next semester, which he was going to spend in Florence, Italy. We talked about this incredible opportunity, about the technology that would allow him to use Skype or Messenger to talk with friends and family over the internet for free. I reminisced about the dark ages I was from. I remember getting our first color TV when I was eight years old, cell phones did not exist until long into my working years (which started in 1985), we had one computer in the office that was for data management, and no one went overseas for a semester of study.

The dark ages have come and gone and today, most colleges encourage and some even require students to study abroad, everyone has at least one smartphone, land-line phones are a thing of the past, computers run everything from our homes to our cars, and I now have fourteen computers in my office. And thirty years from now, today's advances will seem like black and white TVs to us, and we will be in awe at how far we have come. We will wonder how we got along with a cell phone when there is this new gizmo that is integral to our lives some twenty years from now.

The reason for all these changes is *knowledge*. Knowledge is this amazing ability to take what we know today and use it to make small, large, and sometimes miraculous advancements that will forever change how and what we do.

Think about the computer. How this small box, laptop, smart phone, whatever, can hold so much information and be so useful and necessary in our lives is a wonder. And what is the computer based on? Two numbers: one and zero. We learned about one and zero when we were three years old, but someone figured out how to use these numbers to create the digital world. Amazing how it has changed our world in almost every aspect, with lots more to come if we let it.

So, how does this apply to dentistry, or any profession, for that matter? You must, you absolutely must, make life-long learning and the desire to improve your knowledge a crucial piece of your profession. While we are mandated to take a certain amount of continuing education in many professions to maintain our licensure, it is much more involved than that. We must offer our patients the very latest services and materials available, we must adapt our businesses and techniques to improve our outcomes, we must offer new services that improve our patients' oral health, we must train ourselves and our staff, and we must continue to feed our brains, which will drive our energy and excitement for what we do. We must also find new ways to communicate with our patients, especially in this digital world.

In 2014, after over thirty years in practice, I earned my fellowship in the International College of Oral Implantologists after completing an intensive nine-month training program. With the bulk of my practice years behind me, why did I spend so much time and money on this educational opportunity? For me, it was clearly the desire to learn and grow, but it's also where the dental world is headed, and I didn't want to be left behind. Learning new things forces me to stay current, stay sharp, and provide excellent care for my patients. It's also fun.

So what must you do to consistently improve your knowledge base?
1. Take continuing education courses
2. Read professional journals and articles
3. Participate in study clubs
4. Read non-dental books and articles
5. Meet with specialists to learn from them
6. Take webinars
7. Listen to audiobooks, CDs, and podcasts
8. Write

KEY TAKEAWAY: Knowledge is critical for long-term success. Your efforts to learn, teach your staff, and improve your practice will determine your success and happiness in your working world. Staying stagnant will cause a slow, painful death that does not need to happen.

Hand in hand with knowledge is innovation. Every business needs to transform itself on a regular basis. Materials, services, equipment, and technology are changing at a rapid pace, creating better and more improved processes. The way I make a crown for a tooth is completely different today than what I did thirty years ago. I now use a computer to create a digital image and then design and make the crown utilizing the most innovative CAD/CAM technology. And I do it in about an hour, compared to sending an impression to the dental lab and waiting two to three weeks for it to come back. While this has created a better outcome, it has also created a much better patient experience, and it's a lot more fun, too. It's a win-win situation for my practice and for the patient.

> **ACTION STEP:** Think about how many learning and knowledge activities you did in the past. How much reading did you do? How much did you do away from the office? Next, create a monthly knowledge calendar that tracks your reading, web-based learning, and coursework. Better yet, ask a mentor for a book from their library and see what they're doing to stay ahead of the curve.

LOOKING FORWARD

We have all heard the quote, "If you keep doing what you've always done, you'll keep getting what you've always gotten." I'm not sure about you, but I'm not willing to settle for the status quo. Go back to the last chapter, and that should erase your desire to hold on to the past. I couldn't function without my digital x-rays, my CEREC unit, and my 3-D digital scans. How many of you still own a camera that uses film? I have a few big, clunky film cameras sitting on my shelves. You can hardly even find film anymore.

We all remember our parents talking about the good old days and how things were, how much less things cost, and how things were better. If you're old enough, you may be the one saying some of these things. But I hope you see things a little more clearly than that and are willing to commit to changing the future, specifically *your* future.

Let me tell you about Pauline. She's a patient in her late seventies, and she and I have talked NBA basketball and NFL football for twenty-five years. I have done a lot of work for Pauline and had lots of conversations with her, but you can be surprised when people do the unexpected. I was telling Pauline about my son's summer in China and how I used Skype to talk with him in real time via the webcam. She then told me she used Skype and Facebook to keep up with her grandchildren, who live in the US and in Europe. I was surprised by the fact this older woman was using the technology of today for her advantage. I had tried for years to get my father (who would be about Pauline's age) to use the computer for things he liked, but his mindset was not one to look forward, but to maintain the status quo.

So where is your mindset? Are you moving forward or are you settling for the status quo?

> **KEY TAKEAWAY:** Don't let the past prevent you from moving forward. Keep the past in your peripheral vision, but look to the future. In this way, you can move forward, but with the knowledge of where you have come from, now with no limitations except your own. We can and do limit ourselves because we only see the past. While simple, this exercise will help you see beyond the obvious.

Many dental suppliers and manufacturers try to get us to purchase expensive equipment and technology. All of these products are ones we can't do without, or so they say. So, let me tell you about CEREC (a digital crown system) and my experience.

I have always tried to be progressive in staying up with the latest and greatest. But I was never and will never be first. I will let others be the beta test site for companies. I did it once with a computer software company and never again. I was fascinated by CEREC and what it could do, but I couldn't figure out how it would be a major benefit to my practice. The limitations, time constraints, and training were too much for me. But when the latest and much-improved version of CEREC came out, things changed. It became a win-win for both me *and* the patient. Faster design, proven materials, terrific new cements, and cost containment finally all added up. So after two years of looking at it, I added it to my practice in 2006. The benefits have far outweighed the limitations, and I am excited by how I can integrate this into my practice daily. My patients absolutely love it and so do I. It made a crucial piece of my business fun.

Interesting note: In 2018, less than twenty percent of general dentists and prosthodontists are using this CAD/CAM dentistry in their office. While not for everyone, the world is going digital and so is dentistry. I wonder what those numbers will look like in the years to come.

While we don't have crystal balls, in order to stay relevant, we must keep looking forward to the future. We must find ways to energize ourselves and our business, and we must take strategic risks to stay ahead of the curve.

> **ACTION STEP:** Move forward with a purpose. Doing things just to do them or because someone tells you to is foolish and expensive (i.e. a waste of money). Define and write down the things that are important to you and your practice, what the benefits are, and what the ROI (return on investment) is. Once done, you can move forward if it makes sense for you, and find ways to integrate this knowledge and innovation into your practice.

IT'S ALL ABOUT THE RELATIONSHIP

I have touched upon this in almost every chapter so far, but I wanted to give relationships their own little chapter to re-emphasize the importance and value of how they can affect your practice.

Some people are blessed with people skills and some are not. Some have to work at their communication skills and some are naturally gifted. Some people can "read" those around them and others just don't have a clue. Some people are incredibly smart, yet they can do things that are so dumb. Some dentists can have magnificent clinical skills yet be terrible dentists. Some dentists can have gorgeous offices yet struggle to fill them with patients. So, what is the number one factor that will determine your success in dentistry? It's all about relationships.

> **KEY TAKEAWAY:** Ninety-eight percent of what we do in dentistry has nothing to do with our clinical skills. It has everything to do with our relationships with our patients and our staff.

Let me be perfectly clear in stating that our clinical skills are crucial to our success. Being a lousy dentist/salesman and business owner will get you nowhere and may get you in lots of trouble. But our patients have no clue whether our crown margins are perfect or not, or whether we did a great root canal or a lousy one. They have two main concerns: 1) Does it look good, and 2) Did it hurt? They have neither the training nor the experience to make any judgment about anything else. Once you get past these two items, you are down to one key factor, which is whether or not they like you (and your staff).

I recently had a conversation with a nice young woman who wanted cosmetic work to fix some eroded tooth surfaces that were due to acid reflux and some subsequently chipped front teeth. Initially, she was interested in crowns to restore these teeth, and we discussed the pros and cons of this work. She was ready to go, or so I thought. She then did some research online and decided she wanted to preserve as much tooth structure as possible, so the crowns she had wanted were no longer in the plan. We then had a forty-five-minute conversation about making her teeth look beautiful without drilling them or doing anything to them. This conversation was no longer really about teeth, but more about our relationship. This was only our second visit together and she needed reassurance from me that I was the guy to do this work for her. She told me she didn't want her teeth reduced, and I listened. She told me she wanted a great smile, and I listened. She apologized fifteen times for changing her mind, and I listened.

And when she was done talking, she listened. I told her I shared her concerns, but I was the expert, and then I told her why she should do what I recommended. I told her about doing veneers for my wife (oops, secret is out now) and that I would treat her like I would treat my wife. I told her what I would do, including some reduction of her remaining tooth structure. And I told her the only way she could judge me in the end is if she loved the way things looked. End of story. The one thing she needed to give me was her trust to do what was best for her and to make her smile as beautiful as it used to be. Her response was to apologize one more time and make an appointment to get in as quickly as possible. She had no real clue as to how I would technically do her work, but I worked overtime to earn her trust and cement our relationship. Do not underestimate how crucial fostering relationships is to your success in treatment planning, and in the final result. Patients (or customers) who don't trust you will drive you crazy with baseless complaints and see things that don't exist.

We have an automatic survey that's sent to all of our new patients. The responses we get are overwhelmingly great with lots of wonderful praise for our office. But the one thing that's always missing is any mention of our clinical skills. Comments are always about how nice we were, how professional and caring we were, and how accommodating and friendly we were. The one common factor in all the comments is the relationship we established with them from the time they called our office, walked in the front door, and were greeted by a smiling, friendly face, until the moment they paid their bill and left the office. Many of the comments also mention the twenty- to twenty-five years that many of these people have been loyal patients in my practice.

The best way to build relationships is to take time, to make time, to talk to your customers.

I enjoy conversations with my long-time patients, talking about work, family, and vacations. It drives my staff a little crazy as I can sometimes get a little long-winded, but in the end, it makes me feel good, as well as my patients. As I mentioned earlier, it builds loyalty *and* business referrals.

ACTION STEP: What are you and your staff doing that builds relationships with your patients? Think about your patients' experience in your office. Have your entire team spend some time on this. Remember, staff are on the front line and you depend on them. If they aren't doing what you want them to, do something about it. Write down your expectations, help them understand the importance of this process, and hold them accountable.

CONSULTANTS

Question: Where is the best place for your money?
Answer: Your own pocket.

Many business owners, dentists clearly among them, abdicate their roles as leaders and business owners to someone else. But just showing up and providing dental service is not a responsible way to own and run a business. Get the help you need, but also invest time in yourself and in your team to be the leader of your practice.

First, let me be clear—consultants and experts are incredibly knowledgeable and can provide great information to help our practice. But, as an owner, you must be in control. I have learned from the best in dentistry over the years. From the clinical end, I have studied with Christensen, Dawson, Misch, Spear, and many others. From the business side, I have learned from Miles, Levin, Stoltz, and Manji. I have used their information and expertise to help nurture and refine my vision for my practice. I have taken time and worked on it. It is mine to control and I have seized control over every aspect. However, I do not micromanage. As my practice has grown, my approach has changed, but I am the boss. I now share control with my partner, Dr. Tricia Rodney, and an office administrator. We hire great people and give them responsibility for various aspects of our practice, and then oversee what they do. They report to us and we hold them accountable for the things that need to be done. In the end, I take responsibility for everything that goes on in my office, and you must do the same in yours.

Let me go back to consultants and the role they can and should play in your office. Consultants and advisors should be mentors. People with knowledge who can help you craft a well-run business that is profitable and enjoyable are necessary. These people help ground us, help us avoid mistakes, and help us to reduce our stress and become more profitable. They can help steer us in the right direction and save us a lot of time and money. The expression *work smarter, not harder* is particularly applicable here.

KEY TAKEAWAY: You must clearly know what you want to happen when hiring a consultant. Hire a company or person who understands your needs and will work with you on your practice-specific goals. One size does not fit all.

I am relatively creative when it comes to marketing ideas and the design of things like my website and various ads that I place. I like to have final control of the product, but I have hired a great company to give me advice, come up with some unique and successful copy, and design pieces that are stimulating and successful. This is not my area of expertise, but I use these consultants to save me time and make me money. I go over their work and give final sign-off on the finished product before proceeding.

This is again about having control of all aspects of your practice. You can and should define what areas of your practice you want to work on. I think it's impossible to work on all things at the same time. Refer to the goals section again. Define the goals that will most impact your practice and then hire a consultant as needed to help you work on these areas.

All of this led me to create my own dental consulting company. My wife and I have talked for years about helping dentists in a target-specific way, and in 2010, DentalKarma was formed. Our goal is to help teach and train dentists to be their own consultants, where they monitor their practice based on expected outcomes, and then adapt to the circumstances. This will allow practices to respond quickly and more effectively.

My brother Steve is a CPA who used to handle our accounting needs while working for a very large international accounting firm. We really were too small a client, but he kept me on until it was just too ineffective for both of us. But while he was my accountant, he drilled into me the power of being in control of your practice's financial health. Many people spend many hundreds to thousands of dollars a month having an accounting firm do basic bookkeeping practices when they really can do it on their own. Steve taught us to set up our own accounting software, QuickBooks, which could handle all accounting and bill-paying services we would need. He also forced me to be a better steward of my money. Today, we pay our accountants once a year for our corporate and 401k tax returns. And, in the meantime, we get to keep more money in our pockets.

ACTION STEP: Determine if there are areas of your practice where you have given control to someone else. Start to take them back. Meet with the people who control these aspects of your business, and have them help you understand what they are doing and how you can start to manage these areas with their help. If you cannot, then let them do it for you, but be in control. Hire a consultant to teach you how to manage various aspects of your practice. Remember, you are the CEO.

HAVE FUN

My long-time friend and mentor, Dr. Mark Hyman, shared a quote with me years ago that resonates with me each day. He may not remember it, but I imagine it may still guide him as well.

> *"What you need is not what I do."*
> —Dr. Mark Hyman

Mark's quote applies both clinically and managerially. From the clinical end, it means that I do the things I'm great at, and refer out the things that are better in someone else's hands. I do a lot of root canals, but I refer many out when it's in my patient's best interest (and mine) to let a specialist care for them. I do not do third molar extractions. Again, my decision. I love cosmetic work and I love my CEREC unit. CEREC has changed my outlook and how I practice. It is just plain fun and exciting, and it benefits both my patients and me. It does not get any better than that.

The fastest way to not have fun at work is to do things that are too stressful or things you are not great at. I used to do more types of treatment, but found they were not enjoyable and added stress to my days. Better to use the expertise and skills of others to help both my patients and me.

Dentistry, or any career, should be fun. I have a blast with my staff. I sing just to make them smile, and annoy them in a good way. By the way, I cannot sing, but it doesn't stop me from sometimes singing a few notes in a staff meeting or when I pass them in the hall. I write birthday poems that pick on them and are pretty funny. They love it because it's just for them. I make them feel important (remember our quote from chapter two?), I tell crazy stories about past patients, and listen to their crazy ones. And my staff is keenly aware when I'm not having fun. It could be a tough patient or maybe they are not doing what they should, but they sense it and I am sure my patients do as well. I am sure your patients and staff are no different.

Let me tell you about one of my hygienists, who seems to have more fun than anyone. Her patients come back to see her for her conversation and hilarious banter. She usually ends the appointment with something like "get your crap and get out of here." Most people could never get away with it, but she does, and she does it well. In a bizarre way, she makes them feel important, even if she is picking on them and giving them a hard time. They enjoy returning the favor and get in plenty of good jabs, but it's all in fun and that's the key. They wouldn't have her any other way, and neither would she, and it's all about the relationship they have with each other.

As I reflect on my more than thirty years in practice, the defining quality that has made this profession so enjoyable is that I have fun at work. Sometimes it's gut-busting fun, other days it's put-a-smile-on-your-face fun. Very seldom, it's not much fun, but those days are so few and far between I don't count them.

One reality of being a dentist is I go to work every day, and most of the people I treat don't want to be in my office. Some keep it to themselves, and others are quite vocal in proclaiming their hatred for the dental profession. There aren't many people who like the idea of injections, in spite of the fact that they all comment on how easy and painless my shots are. I think a lot of people have heard so many stories about how bad the dentist's office and the dentist can be that they actually convince themselves it's true before giving us a try. But in the end, most people don't mean anything by it and almost always say, "Don't take this personally," and I'm on board with that. I look at this way: at least they come to see me. Don't get caught up with this "hatred" for the dentist. Take advantage of it and show them how good it can be. I always look at it as a challenge, whether the patient is an adult scared by bad experiences from long ago, or a child who's scared by their first appointment in a dental office. For me, and for you, it comes down to having fun.

I am a talker. I love to make small talk, and even will talk politics if you're so inclined. Telling jokes is not off-limits, but I must know the patient really well.

Let me tell you about my friend and patient of twenty-five years, Bill. Bill used to come in and tell me jokes he thought my father would like, even though he had never met my dad. He kind of "met him" through our conversations over the years. I repeated many of those jokes to my dad, who probably wondered who this guy was. But, in reality, my conversations with Bill had very little to do with the jokes and more about having fun with each other.

My staff sometimes runs me out of the room to stay on schedule when the fun goes on too long. I have found that when I hire the right people, they have just as much fun as I do. Basically, we need to lighten up and enjoy ourselves, our staff, and our patients.

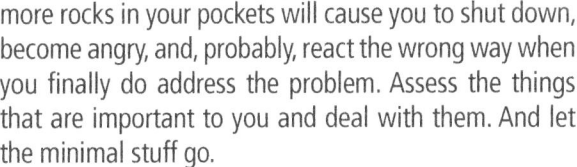

KEY TAKEAWAY: Stop putting "rocks in your pockets." Rocks are things that upset you that you never deal with. These rocks can be things at home or at work, things people say or do, or really almost anything. But putting more rocks in your pockets will cause you to shut down, become angry, and, probably, react the wrong way when you finally do address the problem. Assess the things that are important to you and deal with them. And let the minimal stuff go.

ACTION STEP: Have fun every day. It is absolutely crucial to your life. Make sure fun is a part of both your personal and business worlds. I hope you figure it out and make sure your life is fun. I have it figured out, and I make each and every day one to treasure. And so should you ... Remember, life is just not that complicated!

SO, NOW WHAT?

My goal in writing this book was to create a guide, not a step-by-step process, because life is just not that easy and that structured. My hope is that it will help open up your thoughts and ideas and allow you to be more successful, reach your goals faster, and eliminate some, just some, of the headaches and roadblocks that will surely come.

> *"No matter how many mistakes you make or how slow the progress, you are still way ahead of everyone who isn't trying."*
> –Tony Robbins

Nobody ever said life was easy, but it takes a lot of work to be successful no matter what you do. You can and must determine your path if you want to accomplish your goals. Sometimes it takes longer than you or others expect. That's okay. Remember we all have goals, even if we don't write them down. Those goals can be as simple as wanting to go on vacation to a special place, seeing a sporting event, going to visit family, working for a company, or getting the job of your dreams.

When I was a senior in high school applying to college, the best thing to do, according to my mother, was to have testing done to determine what kind of profession or job you should go into based on aptitude tests. My brother Steve and I went along with it in spite of objections and the fact that we each already knew what we wanted to do. See, Steve and I had it figured out at age fifteen—I wanted to be a dentist and Steve wanted to be an accountant. So, we took the tests to make Mom happy, and then went back for the debriefing and reveal. My test said I should not be a dentist and Steve's said he should not be an accountant. And that was the end of this experiment, because we never went back, we stuck to our desires, worked our tails off, and became who we wanted to be, not what others or some test said we should be. My favorite way to describe this is:

It's much better to order from the menu than to take leftovers.

KEY TAKEAWAY: Aim high and strive to be your best, no matter what that may be. Work hard on yourself and the people around you. Slow down, have fun, and enjoy your life, because you only get one shot at it. And out-work everyone else and let them have the leftovers.

www.ingramcontent.com/pod-product-compliance
Lightning Source LLC
Chambersburg PA
CBHW022107040426
42451CB00007B/165